Rhyming Michigan
Poems About the Great Lakes State

All rights reserved. ISBN: 9798995031826

VM Publications • vincentmoyet.com

Dedicated to all the creative souls
ever to walk the halls of Pine River.

May your work enrich the world,
may your vision never wither.

Rhyming
MICHIGAN

Poems About the Great Lakes State

This is the history told by the folk, so decorated and inflated in the retelling that the core of plain fact is soon swaddled in fancy, and no outsider dare winnow the truth from the fable.

Richard M. Dorson

Contents

Long ago, in what is now Wisconsin,
on Lake Michigan's western shore,
a mother bear and her two cubs
were nestled sleeping on the forest floor.

She had visions in a scary dream
that the woods were burning bright.
She awakened from her slumber
to find darkness pushed by fire's light.

All the woods, all they knew,
burned as far as she could see.
She quickly roused her little cubs,
"Precious souls, follow me."

Through the forest, through the flames,
to water's edge with just one choice;
Mother Bear said to her cubs,
"Swim easterly behind my voice."

They swam into Lake Michigan,
and the moon hid behind the clouds.
The cubs lost sight of Mother Bear,
and darkness covered them in shrouds.

The cubs swam on as distance grew
between themselves and Mother Bear.
They called for her as they swam,
but ahead was only darkness there.

And as the morning light broke out,
Mother Bear sadly knew
she alone was reaching shore -
the Water Mitten came into view.

She crawled atop the dunes
as the sun moved across the sky,
looking out into the water,
she saw her cubs drown and die.

There she stayed to rest in vigil
and watch the water in her grief;
the Spirit gave her rest in slumber
and pulled the sand around her for relief.

And to honor both her little cubs,
the Spirit raised them up as two small islands,
and Mother Bear still rests and watches
as the peaceful sand dune on the highland.

On the shore of Heaven's tip,
along Superior's enchanted sands -
before the Ojibwe met the French -
a maiden stood on the Spirit's land.

She lost her love to the great water -
he died graveless in the greatest lake -
her remaining days she sang to him,
on the beach, for mourning's sake.

And when she passed from this world,
within the sand her song remained,
summoned now by modern folks
to honor her love the water claimed.

Rival to the Thunderbird up high,
Superior's waves live within its eye.
The whirlpool from its mighty tail
has caused many sailing ships to fail.
All the fishes swim away
when Mishipeshu comes their way.
It quickly eats its hunted catch -
a thousand sturgeon in one batch.
And when Mishipeshu drinks with speed,
the Up North rivers all recede.
But the beast is more than big and strong,
a guardian with simple means to get along:
leave the copper by the water,
Mishipeshu does not capture, only slaughter.

In history books it has been scrawled,
at the behest of René de La Salle,
the ship was built near Niagara Falls.

The priests there with him gave him warning,
"Sir, name it not for beast or faerie."
They did not trust the salute to myth,
"Name it for the Saints or Virgin Mary."

La Salle hadn't time for silly omens,
and laughed them off as construction went.
Trading fur and making profit,
not pleasing God, was his intent.

The land was wooded, dense, and thick,
the Seneca came to watch and look,
amazed at the giant in their sight,
in awe of how many trees it took.

Mixed with awe was anger too,
a Native prophet addressed the crew.
Prophecy went through him toward the ship,
and, in a roar, a curse flew from his lips:

"Darkness like a cloud will encompass you,
and the water will claim your great canoe!

The plans aboard will come to spoilage,
Le Griffon will not survive its maiden voyage!"

But La Salle simply ignored this too,
and in his way, boastful and cheery,
finished the body and raised the sails,
and launched Le Griffon in Lake Erie.

West he sailed through Erie fast,
then up the strait, that water sliver -
before Cadillac settled the banks -
known now to us as Detroit River.

The ship arrived on a big lake,
La Salle named it Lake St. Clair,
then over the rapids into Lake Huron,
but, for Huron's gales, was unprepared.

Such storms and tempests of the Lakes
were like none La Salle had ever seen.
Three days tossed at Huron's mercy -
he asked God to intervene.

And soon the waters round them calmed,
and it seemed that they were saved,
they carried on in that grand ship,
they sailed North and sailed unscathed.

With size and guns yet unseen,
Le Griffon reached Michilimackinac,
the size of the vessel, the sound of its guns,
transfixed the Natives by what they saw.

Then Le Griffon sailed Michigan,
sailing West in northern waters,
and finally arrived where it was going,
an island harbor below Escanaba.

La Salle docked the ship for time enough
to load a fortune in fur to haul.
He stayed behind for exploration,
sending the ship, with six men, back to Niagara Falls.

La Salle bid farewell to his ship,
standing, watching, on the shore -
not knowing that Le Griffon left him,
to sink its way so deep into our lore.

Pillaged, stormed, vanished, gone,
unknown the fate of those six souls -
they and Le Griffon were never found,
cruel Lake Michigan took them whole.

But it is said Le Griffon sails,
and a few remain who still believe it;
out on the Lakes in phantom form,
and of the few, only sailors see it.

Jacques loved Genevieve from afar,
though his pursuits were uninvited.
She wanted just to become a nun,
and left his love unrequited.

Genevieve built an altar on the beach,
she placed the Virgin's statue on a stone -
the rock there placed by a Manitou -
where she let her faith be known.

Jacques ventured off to sell his soul,
to where witches dwell in the woods -
he found a crone alone before a fire,
and her shadow danced while she stood.

Jacques implored the witch,
"Give me old magic from Normandy!
I need Genevieve by fair or foul -
ancient witch, take my soul and hear my plea!"

Then the fire blazed up straight and bright,
the witch screamed in laughter crying high -
the love of taking souls consumed her,
and she put his spirit madly in her eye.

Jacques went forth without his soul,
but new power flowed in him.
He could, with thought, not be human,
and become a werewolf on a whim.

Before long, Jacques found the altar.
From the thicket, he could keenly see
Genevieve was alone and praying,
before Mary's statue on bended knee.

This was his chance, she would be his,
the girl prayed silent and alone -
but when Jacques jumped out from the woods,
the Virgin's statue turned him into stone.

Part One, 1701

On the land once called New France,
a hall of nobles from way back,
sat at a banquet up in Québec,
to honor a man named Cadillac.

And for the entertainment of the guests,
some of France's finest and best dressed,
a fortune teller to amuse them all,
was led by a servant into the hall.

A restless figure, tall and dark,
tossed in shadows that forewent her,
wearing garments long and drab,
and a black cat upon her shoulder.

The room inhaled as she entered,
but she went on, remaining calm;
she approached Cadillac at his table,
"Sir, please let me read your palm."

He gave his hand upturned to her,
remaining in his seat.
She said, *"You have conquered Mackinac,
the place where Waters meet.*

*Now you head to the southern straits,
you're chasing new exploits -
you're on your way to settle the river,
which will bear the name Detroit."*

Then the lady dressed in black
said this more to Cadillac:

*"Your city will grow in number
far above what New France now holds;
many children will nestle your hearth,
and you will have the gift of growing old."*

The fortune teller had more to say,
she traced his palm with eyes closed shut,
*"Tests come to all of us,
even you, no matter what!*

*And on these lines your future says
the Nain Rouge might cross your path!
Appease the creature, pay him respect,
appease the thing, and do not laugh!*

He is the demon of the strait,
come to this land from our old State!
And crossing him is a mistake,
for he leaves havoc in his wake.

His skin is wrinkled, red as embers,
with glowing eyes and fangs for teeth,
he is a sight one always remembers,
a sight one hopes to never meet.

Pay him no mind at your own peril,
your colony will scarcely know your name.
Englishmen will take it from France;
a chief named Pontiac will take your fame."

And there will be tumult in Detroit,
whenever the Nain Rouge appears!"
Then the banquet abruptly ended,
and all left shocked by the seer.

Part Two, 1707

Much time had passed since that night -
it was spring in the month of May.
Far from Québec, Detroit was growing,
and springtime fun was underway.

The trading post was prospering well,
then one night, while walking home,
Cadillac and his wife encountered
the little dwarf, the fated gnome!

The Nain Rouge jumped before their path,
he meanly snarled, and then he laughed!

Cadillac was far too proud.
Cadillac could not stay calm.
His wife called out, shrill and scared,
"Think of the writing on your palm!"

The demon laughed louder yet,
then asked if they fancied to see a trick,
but Cadillac doubted who he met,
and beat the dwarf with his walking stick.

Shrieking deathly howls into the night,
the Nain Rouge hopped off in the dark,
and Cadillac's own eyes would never see
the extent to which this left its mark.

What great yarns have been spun for him!
The tales go on from fire bright to fire dim!

Did he live? Was he real?
Is he myth or simple fact?
Was he 12 feet when he kneeled?
What do we know, to be exact?

I heard his footsteps made trees shake,
and that his prints could leave a lake!

What they say, if it's true,
is that his ox was really blue!

Rumor went his liquor was kerosene,
though a Bunyan hangover was never seen.

Camp cooks made flapjacks day and night,
and Paul could eat them stacked to his height!

Someone said he fought a witch,
and that he tamed the AuSable River!
Truth or lore, does it matter which?
Paul's name, in time, has not withered.

Of all the fellers, Paul was the best!
And at the fire, I was told
that Paul outdid all the rest,
known as the king of green gold.

When Mr. Bunyan swung his ax,
"Timber!" cried the shanty boys,
rollin' logs down to the river,
tellin' tales for pleasant noise.

This is a story of foul play in the dark,
of an affair and murder by Seidman Park.

A marriage in silence had found its death,
and the Mrs. took a secret lover -
on full moons they rendezvoused
and met protected by night's cover.

One full moon the Mr. woke -
it was the middle of the night.
His wife was gone but he had a hunch
that something really wasn't right.

He went back to bed, saying nothing,
he feigned sleep when she returned.
The next full moon he was onto her,
but she crept out, unconcerned.

Suspicion led him to the woods,
and there, with a man from out of town,
his wife - unfaithful, though looking happy -
was making love upon the ground.

The lovers stirred, they had no words,
the Mr. pulled his knife.
A tussle ensued, screams pierced the woods,
and the Mr. killed his wife.

The lover lunged with a knife his own
and cut the Mr. to the bone.

The two men fought back and forth,
cutting each other round after round,
until both collapsed from loss of blood,
and turned to corpses on the ground.

Now three souls are trapped forever
in those woods where they were hewn,
now they're summoned like waves to shore,
by the compulsion of the moon.

So when the moon is round and bright,
be weary of the woods by Seidman Park.
You might encounter both tryst and fight,
of those three ghosts trapped in the dark.

A witch once lived alone in the woods,
but her life was violently cut short.
Nearby folk sentenced her to death
without charges or a court.

They trapped her in her house
and with torches marched it round,
then set fire to the cottage
and burned it to the ground.

The marauders watched in the light of fire,
and, from inside, she cursed the land,
"Let life be death that travels here,
let no homestead ever stand!"

And for a while, the land stood alone,
at the end of a two-track tunnel of trees.
The nearby folk feared the curse,
and they stayed away with ease.

But one day, years beyond the witch's death,
when real fear had turned to lore,
a happy family came to Dansville,
and found a piece of land that they adored.

They built a home, large and grand,
with seven gables and a porch.
They defied the curse said by the witch,
and lost themselves to Fate's course.

The father quickly went insane,
and sadly entered this here fable.
He hanged himself from a tree,
but first he hanged his children from the gables.

The grand old house stands no more,
but the legend haunts the land -
there is empty acreage out in Dansville,
cursed to life, let life be damned.

I am now an old sailor,
tempest tossed and well traveled.
I've seen magic on the Lakes -
wind called up by rope unraveled.

I, in my youth of good Port Huron,
was but a cabin boy, fresh and eager,
working for the love of water,
as my wage was low and meager.

I had employment with an old-world captain,
a vintage man with a new schooner,
which once on Michigan was sitting still;
when Nature slowed, the captain acted sooner.

The day was windless on the Lake,
the sun made diamonds on its face -
there was beauty in the calmness
of sitting still in one place.

Captain came to deck with mystic tool,
a knotted rope wrapped round his hand -
he let loose a single not,
a breeze came rushing from the land.

Then another knot untied,
the rope was growing longer,
the breeze became a wind,
the wind grew fast and stronger.

Then the schooner briskly sailed -
the captain's deed was done -
and I, the youth alone,
was awed beneath the glowing sun.

There is a house in lamentation,
a house whose cedars weep,
a mansion and a mausoleum,
with ghosts who roam the grounds they keep.

A young mother lost her baby,
who was buried in the tomb,
and when the funeral was over,
to daily life the house resumed.

But the mother froze in time,
she succumbed to her new plight -
she held and rocked her baby's body,
and left candles burning through the night.

While all the house gently slept,
she snuck off to ease her pain;
the baby's corpse brought no relief,
she lost her mind and went insane.

She soon died, and now it's said
the estate still cries and moans.
Some dismiss it, but others say
there is a haunting in that home.

Off Old 45 there is a light,
above the treeline, atop the ridge.
It can be seen most clear nights,
just stand before the washed out bridge.

They say a ghost is roaming still,
left over from the lumber days.
It's said he was on the job when killed -
stuck forever in those old ways.

He was a railroad worker way back then -
now walks the valley by the power lines,
searching for tracks long since lost,
while his lantern waves ghostly signs.

Up North by Tahquamenon,
a train is rather clearly heard -
around twilight, between dusk and dawn -
the ghost of Con Culhane in the woods.

He was the roughest, toughest lumber boss,
and his wife, Ellen, kept the books.
Felling timber made them money,
and every chance he had he took.

He never missed, and far exceeded,
every month, the company quota,
sending others to find new land
in Wisconsin and Minnesota.

It was the booming timber years,
and to go with standard saw and ax,
Con Culhane had his day's finest,
he had the use of railroad tracks.

But one sad day, out in the woods,
he died beneath his own train.
Ellen buried him and went back to work,
and worked her way through the pain.

Ellen stayed Up North and kept the books,
and with the company stayed engaged,
until time came to leave the region,
at the end of Michigan's Lumber Age.

And now Up North by Tahquamenon,
a train is rather clearly heard -
around twilight, between dusk and dawn -
the ghost of Con Culhane in the woods.

The school bus quiets when the song begins,
it's the tale from old time lumber days;
the little ones quiver up to their chins,
the driver drives, the dogman's story plays.

Or it happens by the light at camp
coming from the flickering flame,
elder folks tell the tales
of the dogman with no name.

With sharp white fangs to kill,
and bright red eyes to see,
he lurks within the woods,
and by the river, Manistee.

Once he prowled outside of Luther,
once he killed a priest.
A North Bar regular claimed to see him,
and reported an eight foot beast.

One time up near a town called Tustin,
a schoolhouse lost its door.
In the morning, the kids stayed home,
there was a mangled deer on the floor.

Farmers have said
they found horses dead;
against this dog, they had no fight,
nor could they run, they died of fright!

And all throughout the northern woods,
when he hunts you'll hear the sound -
his growl strikes fear in the fiercest folks -
like hearing courage being drowned.

But worry just a little less,
read again and hold your fear,
for the dogman only comes
once a decade in the seventh year.

There are some folks in Michigan,
ordinary like you and me.
Except they have a special gift
that nobody can see.

They need no training, no rite of passage,
the gift is theirs, used as they please.
They might be rich or poor, man or woman,
and they pop up in random family trees.

We are unaware of who they are -
they're always closer than we know,
could be a neighbor, local, sibling, parent -
they're never far, wherever we might go.

Once near Munising,
two lads got drunk and had a fight,
an argument first, then, in a flash,
one slashed the other with his knife.

He stumbled, gushing blood,
down the road, into the bar.
Archie stopped the blood with prayer,
then he said, *"That's going to leave a scar."*

This one time, in Lake County,
a man named Wright was threshing wheat.
The band cutter cut him, and cut him good,
it turned his hand to strings of meat.

His cousin Cal rushed him off,
off to the doctor, going fast,
when on the way they saw old Georgie,
who said to them, *"That bleeding will not last."*

And surely, as old Georgie said,
the mangled hand no longer bled.

Some say Georgie always knew,
some say he was taught.
One thing Wright knew was true:
Georgie stopped the blood with just a thought!

This one lumberjack out on Drummond,
knew an Alberta boy with the command,
could stop the bleeding from any wound,
he need only wave his hand.

And there are even some who say
that when the healing is acquired -
after the stoppers perform their task -
a little bit of penance is required.

So be it prayer, waves, or simple thoughts,
lives are saved with stoppers in the room.
Whichever method, the end is the same,
they stop flowing blood from mortals' wounds.

There was lightning in the sky
and waves pounding on the deck -
the schooner struggled in the storm
and succumbed itself to wreck.

They released the yawls,
they abandoned ship -
but fierce Lake Michigan
caused their yawls to tip.

So they swam, the doomed crew,
directionless - nowhere to reach -
until they saw a greenish light
bobbing steadily on the beach.

The sailors swam on hard,
they made it to the sand -
but the light soon quickly vanished,
once they stepped foot upon the land.

The silver moonlight touched a lighthouse,
it's lamp darkened and unlit -
St. Martin's Light that could have saved them,
had St. Martin's Light been lit.

On the sailors went to see
who was derelict that night -
they walked right in to an empty house,
except on the table was the light!

The light that had just saved them,
with not a person to be found;
the sailors called out loud in greeting,
but, except their voices, heard no sound.

The keeper's coat was on the wall,
and they could see it plain -
when they touched the oilskin,
it was dry, untouched by rain.

The sailors ran throughout the house,
they found the keeper long since dead -
decaying in the unlit lighthouse,
the keeper died asleep in bed.

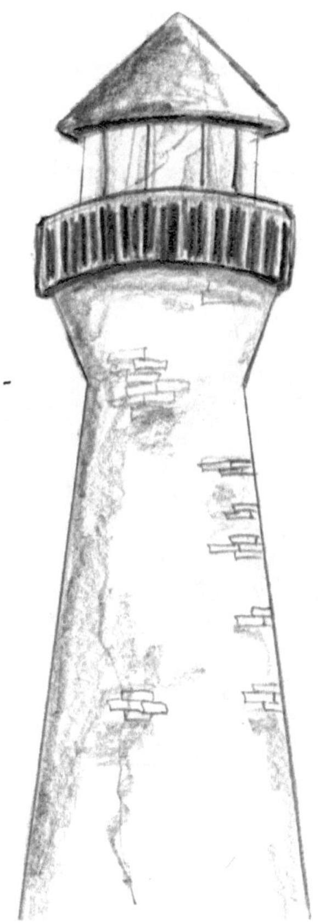

They walk in skin not their own,
not skin of humankind.
They transform themselves in fire,
and have their species reassigned.

They take the form of woodland bears,
they are corrupted healers with ill will,
and it's said the only ones who see them
are those the walkers plan to kill.

I am a sailor with a heavy heart.
A sailor's life gave me all I gained -
memories, home, and income -
my deepest scar and greatest pain.

My wife and I had one son,
and he became a sailor too.
I retired at his beginning,
my time ended with his first crew.

In his spare time he was a diver,
and retrieved an anchor from a wreck.
He gifted it to his mom and me,
and we ornately put it on our deck.

I was enjoying my retired days
and sunsets with my wife -
but then one day news came to us,
the Lake laid claim to our son's life.

Life went on, but we were changed,
the heavy sadness clung to us.
Sadness came to us like silence,
and our son was less and less discussed.

Then one day, while on the lake -
I was fishing all alone -
a seagull swooped and cawed at me,
urging me to hurry home.

I found my wife had fallen down,
she was unconscious on the deck,
but the seagull calmy perched
on the anchor from the wreck.

My wife woke up and sat upright,
the seagull cawed as she came to -
I looked at her, she looked at me,
might a sailor's myth be true?

Since that day, things have improved,
and though the sadness hasn't ceased,
the Great Lakes bird still visits us,
and when it comes, it shows us peace.

Way Up North in the Landmark Inn:
a room with lilac prints upon the wall,
a haunted room that even empty
gives the concierge a call.

The story says a local lady
only stayed in the lilac room.
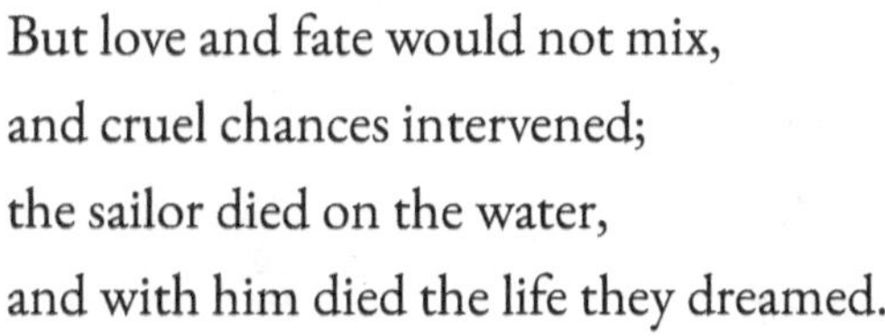
There she'd rendezvous with her lover,
a sailor she thought would be her groom.

But love and fate would not mix,
and cruel chances intervened;
the sailor died on the water,
and with him died the life they dreamed.

With broken heart and broken soul,
she tied knots with shaking hand,
she hated life for the love it stole,
let her remaining years be damned.

Love itself made her life brief,
and it was love that brought her doom;
with sailing rope to aid her grief,
she hanged herself in the lilac room.

Imagine two peninsulas of ancient land,
where water reflected endless wood,
from shore to shore sunbeams danced
down to where the forests stood -
unbroken bark by ax or saw -
old like Eden that He made good.

Then history came to change the world
with Jesuits, who wrote things down,
and explorers bearing charters
to seize land for an old crown
by building posts and forts to live and trade,
while plucking furs and pelts from the ground.

Thus began an evanescence -
in a world that got called new -
of nations old and steeped in time -
in the way of ambition's view -
who fought and hosted Europe's wars,
until our Stars and Stripes raised and flew.

There was destiny to be manifested,
there were cities rising toward the sky -
the woods in Michigan were green gold,
and shanty boys were getting by
while barons slept in pretty mansions,
and whole forests quickly died.

Then desolation swept the land,
leaving plains of stumps behind alone;
and one day a pair arrived
to vanished woods the past had known -
moved by loss and restoration,
they built a shrine where pines had grown.

A cozy cabin by the river,
the pair lived with the land;
as the Modern Age was marching on,
they worked and whittled with their hands;
and trees rose vast again in Michigan,
let them rise and forever stand.

BEHIND THE POEMS

There are two versions of the Anishinaabe story of Sleeping Bear, both serving the same function, which is to explain the geography around Sleeping Bear Dunes National Lakeshore. Both versions of the story begin in what is now Wisconsin. In one version, a famine causes Mother Bear and her two cubs to swim across Lake Michigan in search of food. In the other version, a forest fire drives them into the water. In both versions, Mother Bear reaches the shore in Michigan alone, and she watches her cubs drown. Both versions of the story conclude with the Great Spirit immortalizing the cubs as North and South Manitou Islands and then transforming Mother Bear into the large sand dune that attracts endless visitors to this day.

There is a stretch of sandy shore along Lake Superior in Bete Grise, Michigan on the Keweenaw Peninsula. The local legend says that a young Native American girl lost her love to Lake Superior and spent her days thereafter singing from the beach, where her voice remains. Visitors still make the sand sing by scuffing their heels along the beach or rotating the palms of their hands on the surface. In the legend of Sleeping Bear, the story functions as an explanation for geographical landmarks, whereas the function here is to explain the sound we hear when we scuff sand.

Mishipeshu is a giant water panther in the Native traditions around the Great Lakes. Mishipeshu's home was believed to be Michipicoten Island in the Canadian waters of Lake Superior. Mishipeshu was revered by the Ojibwe of the upper Great Lakes Region, known as a guardian of the copper in Michigan's Upper Peninsula. A copper rush began on the Keweenaw Peninsula and around Isle Royale in the 1840s, but there is evidence that copper had been mined there far earlier, before the presence of Europeans. There is no doubt, however, that the explosive copper rush of the 19th Century extracted more in less time than ever before. Warnings that taking copper from the region angered Mishipeshu have persisted for ages, and the water panther has been given credit for many tragedies that befell vessels carrying the metal both before and after the start of the colonial era.

Le Griffon, a ship for fur trading, was built by French explorer René Cavelier, Sieur de La Salle in 1679. Depending on the source, Le Griffon was the first or second vessel of its size and capacity to sail on the Great Lakes. It did not survive its maiden voyage, and a great deal of what we know about Le Griffon comes to us from translations of journal entries and articles written by Father Hennepin, a missionary who accompanied La Salle and sailed on Le Griffon before it sank.

Made out of timber from the building site by Niagara Falls, the ship was built to enable fur trading with the Natives of the upper Great Lakes. Stories about the building of Le Griffon depict La Salle as boastful and very ambitious, ignoring the concerns of the pious in his company, who advised he name the ship for the Virgin Mary or one of the Saints (as opposed to a mythical, non-Christian creature). The process was also fast, as La Salle was fearful that Natives might burn it. Construction started on the ship in January of 1679, and it was in Lake Erie by early August. Furthermore, there is an account of the ship's building in which an Iroquois prophet, Metiomek, addressed La Salle and foretold the ship's sinking due to La Salle's great pride. La Salle ignored this holy person just as he had ignored his own.

From Lake Erie, La Salle and his company of more than 30 men sailed up the Detroit River into Lake St. Clair and through the St. Clair River (both of which he named) before arriving at Lake Huron. After passing through the Straits of Mackinac, Le Griffon sailed atop Lake Michigan, over to Wassekiganeso Island (now Washington Harbor at the entrance of Green Bay), where a fortune in fur was awaiting him for pickup. La Salle sent Le Griffon back to his port at Niagara Falls with a crew of just six men. La Salle and Father Hennepin were not on board for the return part of the voyage. The ship, the crew, and the fur vanished. Many theories emerged surrounding the fate of the ship, with many plausible possibilities. Whether the ship succumbed to a storm, wreck, mutiny, or pirates, Le Griffon has lived on in mariner lore, and it is widely regarded as the first ghost ship on the Great Lakes.

Independent trappers and traders, known as coureurs de bois (French for "wood runners"), preceded major settlements and forts around the Great Lakes Region. Before Cadillac founded Detroit in 1701, coureurs de bois were living in the area. Genevieve, the daughter of a coureur de bois living by Lake St. Clair, was awaiting word from the Ursuline Convent in Québec, where she hoped to move and spend her life as a nun. Also living in the area was a Frenchman named Jacques Morand, who had been part of the explorer Duluth's company that founded the short-lived Fort St. Joseph on the St. Clair River in 1686.

When he saw her from a distance, Jacques fell immediately in love with Genevieve. Of course, she was not interested, since she considered herself already married to God. Jacques did not handle rejection well, and sought the help of a witch living out in the woods. The witch gave him the ability to transform himself, at will, into a loup garou (French for "werewolf") and then back again.

Meanwhile, Genevieve and her father built an altar on the beach of Lake St. Clair. They placed a statue of the Virgin Mary upon a great rock tossed ashore by a Manitou, and this is where Genevieve spent most of her time, waiting for her letter from the convent. Some versions of the story make no special mention of the rock being placed on the beach by a Manitou. Some do, however, and it adds a greater layer of depth to the story by showcasing the blending of the spiritual traditions of the Native Americans with the spiritual traditions of

Catholic Europeans at a time when the Great Lakes Region was undergoing extreme demographic changes.

One day, when Genevieve was standing at her altar, Jacques pounced from the bushes as the werewolf, intent on having Genevieve, fair or foul. She heard him jump out of the thicket in time to see him and leap out of his way. When Jacques landed where Genevieve had been standing, he was face to face with the statue of the Virgin Mary, and the werewolf was instantly turned to stone.

Le Nain Rouge (French for "the red dwarf") is known as the demon of the straits (referring to the Detroit and St. Clair Rivers that connect Lakes Huron and Erie), and it has enjoyed a regular occurrence in Detroit's folklore and storytelling since the city's founding in 1701. The premise of the Nain Rouge is appeasement. It is said that it appears and goes unappeased by Detroit's inhabitants before disaster strikes. There are stories that claim the Nain Rouge was spotted before the Battle of Bloody Run at the beginning of Pontiac's War, and there are claims the Nain Rouge was spotted before the great Detroit Fire of 1805.

The story behind the poem here deals with how the Nain Rouge came to dwell in Detroit. In popular storytelling, the Nain Rouge was imported from France at the start of the colonial era and has a special connection to Detroit's founder, Antoine Laumet de la Mothe, Sieur de Cadillac. What is historically true is that Cadillac, because of his military service in France, was made commander of Michilimackinac, which controlled the fur trade between the Great Lakes Natives and Europe. Because of his success at Michilimackinac, Cadillac was put in charge of a new fort, which would be established in 1701 as Fort Pontchartrain du Détroit. The fable inserts itself into the history during the period that falls between Cadillac's command of Michilimackinac and his command of Detroit.

The story goes that there was a send-off banquet held in Cadillac's honor up in Quebec the night before he left to found Fort Pontchartrain in 1701. For entertainment, a fortune teller, or sorceress in some accounts, was brought into the banquet hall, and she had an alarming message for Cadillac. The fortune teller revealed that he would encounter the Nain Rouge (whose reputation Cadillac was already familiar with), and if he failed to appease the creature, his children would not receive inheritance and the city he was about to found would scarcely remember his name. Unalarmed, Cadillac goes about his life. Six years later, the earliest iteration of Detroit was thriving, when, one night while walking home with his wife, the Nain Rouge jumped across Cadillac's path. His wife, being more superstitious than he, warmed him to heed the words of the fortune teller, but Cadillac hit the Nain Rouge with his cane instead. Due to what is called "Cadillac's folly," the Nain Rouge has been with Detroit ever since.

Paul Bunyan appears in folklore all throughout the United States, and stories about his exploits reach far and wide. While he has surely traveled, Paul Bunyan belongs to Michigan. There is conjecture that a historical person stands behind Paul Bunayan, though, the actual lumberjack serving as the basis changes depending on who is making the conjecture. There are also many claims as to when Paul Bunyan first emerged in the American psyche, but, in general, there is consensus that he entered the oral storytelling tradition of late 19th Century lumber camps, and then later found his way into print in the early decades of the 20th Century.

Ada Township was organized out of a late-blooming trading post right around the same time Michigan gained statehood. The local legend says that the love had fallen away from an Ada couple's marriage. The wife took a lover, whom she would meet in the middle of the night while her husband slept. Soon enough, the husband grew suspicious. One night, he pretended to fall asleep and followed her when she left. He discovered the affair, and, in a rage, killed her. The lover then attacked him, and the two men engaged in a knife fight that left them both to succumb to their wounds. It is said that the ghosts of all three can be seen around Seidman Park and Findlay Cemetery when the moon is full. People who have claimed to see them report a horrible vision of a woman bleeding out on the ground while two men stab each other to death.

Dansville, Michigan boasts the most haunted road in the state. Seven Gables Road, off E. Dexter Trail, dead ends at an old, rusty gate. Beyond the gate is vast, uninhabited woods. Local legend says that a witch once lived on the land. She met her end when a band of marauders trapped her in her house and set it on fire. As she burned inside the house, the witch called out a curse - that the land would remain unlivable. Years later, a family built a home on the land, presumably either unaware of the curse or in defiance of locals' warnings. In time, the father went insane and hanged his children from the gables of the house before hanging himself from a tree. Today, lost on that 5,000 acres, the foundation of an old house peeks out from the undergrowth, and it is said that those who trespass beyond the rusty gate at the end of Seven Gables Road risk hearing a soul-piercing scream, the omen of death.

Sailors have made vast contributions to storytelling no matter where they appear in history. This story comes from a young Michigan cabin boy from Port Huron who onced sailed with an "old-world" captain heading to the then quickly-rising Chicago. According to the young sailor, Great Lakes captains who immigrated from Europe during the 19th Century were often rumored to have supernatural abilities. In this case, the young cabin boy recounts a story about the schooner being stopped dead in the water due to a lack of wind on Lake Michigan. The captain emerged on deck with a knotted rope, which he untied in order to summon the wind.

There is a mansion in Niles, Michigan that was purchased by lawyer Strother Beeson around 1850. Mr. Beeson built a mausoleum by the mansion when his mother, Judith, passed away. Later, in 1869, his grandson was also buried in the tomb as an infant. Mr. Beeson's daughter-in-law, Harriet, never recovered from the death of her baby, and it is said that she returned to the crypt in the night. She held, rocked, and talked to the baby's corpse until its decomposition caused Harriet to go insane. It is said that she was institutionalized.

In the Ottawa National Forest, between Watersmeet and Paulding, there is a stretch of Old US 45 that sits off in the woods to the west of current US 45. Robbins Pond Road, off 45, leads to a guardrail that overlooks a valley with power lines running through it along the old highway. Nearly every night, mysterious lights appear over the treeline on the horizon. People have shared different experiences with the light. Sometimes it's one orb, sometimes it's two. Sometimes it rises or falls, sometimes it zooms at the spectator(s), and sometimes it merely lingers before vanishing. Crowds regularly gather at dusk to experience the phenomenon. The Forest Service even placed a sign declaring the spot a viewing area. According to the sign, the light is from the lantern of an old railroad worker's ghost, who died on the job, but still shows up faithfully to light the way.

Cornelius (Con) Culhane was a lumber boss in the Tahquamenon region at the turn of the century. Con and his wife, Ellen, dominated the timber between the Little Two Hearted and Tahquamenon Rivers, all around Newberry, and up Whitefish Bay. Their lumber company kept the sawmill in Shelldrake (now a ghost town) fully operational and very busy. The Culhanes had the reputation for sending other lumber companies out of the Upper Peninsula, off to Minnesota and Wisconsin, to find timber. Eventually, the Culhanes started their own railroad logging company. It operated from 1893 until Con's death in 1903. Con Culhane was crushed by one of his own engines, and people never stopped hearing Con Culhane's train in the woods.

Like so many of the historical figures mentioned in this book, some combination of the Culhanes' reputation, way of life, failures, and accomplishments, has lifted them from the history books' pages and placed them into great local and regional fame. The following is from a Newberry, Michigan newspaper - Friday, July 3, 1903:

Wealthy Lumberman Thrown Under Car Wheels At Shelldrake - Well Known Here

Con Culhane, the well known lumberman, was killed instantly by a logging train Friday while riding in a car on one of his own tracks near Shelldrake.

He was killed so quickly that it was hard to tell just what happened. The train was running at a good rate of speed and the brakeman was uncoupling from the engine when it happened. Culhane was on the end of the car watching the man and as the engine slacked back suddenly to allow the brakeman to pull the pin, the car was checked suddenly and pitched forward and went under the wheels. It was impossible to stop the car, so sudden was the fall.

The remains were first taken to the Soo to be prepared for burial, and from there to Port Austin where the funeral was held. Deceased came originally from the Saginaw valley and has many friends in that part of the state. Con Culhane was one of the most prominent figures in the commercial life of the upper peninsula. He came to this country without a cent and amassed a large fortune. It is stated that he was easily a millionaire, and according to the opinion of men who were acquainted with him he had more ready money than any man in the state. All the lands around Shelldrake were owned by him and he had a large number of men in his employ.

His logging railroad was one of the best equipped in the country and his plant did an enormous business.

Mr. Culhane was a man about 61 years of age and leaves a wife and son. He was well known among the business men of Newberry, and was universally respected. When the news of his tragic death came people were greatly shocked and the affair was the subject of much conversation.

By his untimely passing away the business circles of the state will lose one of the men who have had much to do with the development of the upper peninsula. He saw that there was money to be made in this part of the state and applied himself to the end that he might build up a great industry on the shores of Whitefish Bay. It is stated by many that he intended retiring from active business life in the near future to enjoy the fruits of his labor in well earned rest. He was taken away just at a time when he was contemplating taking things easy.

The Michigan dogman was popularized by a DJ from Traverse City named Steve Cook. Cook's song "The Legend" (1987) still enjoys widespread circulation on the radio around Halloween. The song tells the story of a half dog, half man creature that stalks the northwest woods of the Lower Peninsula. According to "The Legend", the dogman appears once a decade in the seventh year. The song details accounts of dogman sightings dating back to 1887. Cook admitted to making up the story, but anecdotal accounts still popped up, people claiming to have seen the dogman prior to 1987. Cook also acknowledged that he used Michigan folklore as well as hunting stories for inspiration, thus placing his biped legend within a long lasting Michigan tradition of such tales.

In 1946, Professor Richard M. Dorson left his office at Indiana University to embark on a five month journey into the Upper Peninsula. The Mackinac Bridge was not yet built, so Dorson crossed the Straits by ferry to discover and collect folklore from the U.P. Dorson characterized his five month excursion into the Upper Peninsula as a microcosm of American folklore in general, defined by three great influences: Native American oral traditions, European immigration during the previous century, and the work and ways of American life.

Dorson encountered several stories about healers with the ability to stop the flow of blood. Most of the accounts told to Dorson by U.P. residents are set in the U.P., but there are a few in the mix that are recounted as having happened in the Lower Peninsula and Canada. A byproduct of these far-reaching stories is little consistency. The method a bloodstopper uses varies from story to story; it appears as a prayer, incantation, gesture, and a mere thought. Similarly, the way in which a bloodstopper receives the gift varies from story to story. Some say a man can teach a woman, others say a woman must teach a man. Some reports claim the gift is the effect of a baby born with placenta on its face. Some say it is hereditary. Accounting for all the variations, what remains true is that the people telling the stories did not all know one another, and they were separated by great distances and spans of time.

St. Martin Island sits in the small archipelago that is strung between the U.P.'s Garden Peninsula and Wisconsin's Door Peninsula. The St. Martin Light was first lit in 1905, and, like so many other Michigan lighthouses, has contributed its fair share of ghost stories to the state's lore.

A prevailing account of a ghostly encounter is that of a time when the lighthouse's lamp went unlit. That same night, a violent storm rolled over Lake Michigan, and a ship went down within swimming distance of the island. Thankfully, all the crew members made it to shore with the help of a little green light that bobbed around the beach and guided them to it. When the whole crew was safe on land, the light disappeared. The sailors made their way through the ongoing storm to the darkened lighthouse that, had it been lit, could have prevented the whole disaster. They entered the living quarters of the lighthouse and found a gently burning lantern on the table, and there was a dry coat hanging on the wall. The captain called out into the house, but he received no response. The sailors wandered around and found the lightkeeper deceased in his bed.

Like the bloodstoppers, the bearwalkers found their way into this book via Dorson's five month excursion in the U.P. In some versions, a person transforms into a bear in a flash, or in a fire, and it is a bad omen for any person who witnesses this. In some instances, there is an evil "medicine" involved that brings about death, and in others simply seeing the walker is enough. Then there are accounts in which the evil person (the walker) might not be a bear at all, but an owl, coyote, or even a beetle. In some versions, the walkers keep pieces of their victims' bodies, and in others they retrieve the medicine they administered so it can be used again. The stories surrounding bearwalkers are riddled with even more inconsistencies than the bloodstoppers. In all cases, though, seeing a bearwalker is not a good thing, and almost always an indication of coming death.

While seagulls are often disliked by beachgoers, it is a common superstition among sailors that seagulls contain the souls of drowned sailors and offer guidance. Encountering a seagull at the right moment could be a good omen for a person who lives life with the water. In *Spooky Michigan*, S.E. Schlosser tells the story of a small sailing family - a man, wife, and their son. The wife stayed at home with the boy while the father sailed the Great Lakes, eventually making his way up the St. Lawrence River and out onto the ocean. When the son grew up, he also became a sailor, and his career began around the same time his father retired. The young sailor worked on a Great Lakes freighter, and avoided the ocean. He was deeply fascinated with the Great Lakes, and early in his career gifted his parents an old, rusted anchor he retrieved from a shipwreck.

One day, after spending a pleasant day of retirement fishing, the old sailor returned home to find his wife standing alone on their dock. By the look on his wife's face, the old sailor knew their son was gone. He had been swept off his freighter and drowned in Lake Michigan. As they grieved on the dock, a seagull flew through the front of their house, out a back window, and landed before them on the anchor their son had given them. The seagull's presence brought the couple great comfort. The comfort lasted for just that brief moment, and they went on with their lives carrying great sadness.

Not long after, the retired sailor was out in his small boat, fishing on the lake. The seagull flew over frantically, flying and cawing in a way to grab his attention. The sailor had a sinking feeling and knew his wife was in trouble. He rushed home and found her unconscious. She had fallen off the deck while watering flowers. The seagull landed on the old anchor and watched over the woman as her husband phoned for help. As help arrived, the seagull flew away. The couple never saw the seagull again, but lived their days without the sadness. The poem in this book veers slightly from this story, but preserves the small family, the loss of the son, and the aid of the seagull.

The Landmark Inn opened in Marquette in 1930. With stunning views of Lake Superior, it was the center of the social scene in Marquette, with notable guests that included Amelia Earhart, Abbott and Costello, Jim Harrison, astronaut Jerry Linenger, as well as other artists, writers, politicians, and businessmen. The hotel fell into disrepair and closed in 1982, but soon after was revived and reopened in 1995.

One of Marquette's most famous ghost stories comes from the Landmark Inn. The story goes that a local librarian used the Inn as a rendezvous location to meet her lover, who was a sailor. They met in the lilac room, named for its pretty wallpaper. One day, the sailor never arrived, and she later discovered that his ship went down in Lake Superior. Overcome with grief, she hanged herself in the lilac room.

In the second half of the 19th Century, Michigan's trees, particularly the white pine, created more millionaires than all the gold in the California Gold Rush. The wilderness of the Great Lakes State had been brooding on the peninsulas since the Ice Age, but the lumber barons saw the primeval landscape as a pathway to progress and wealth. Acreage was cheap and timber was booming, a driving force behind the rising infrastructure in the quickly growing United States. A standard lumber camp had 70 men or more, yokes of oxen, and teams of horses. There was a kitchen shanty, bunkhouse, blacksmith, carpenter, and a store for clothes and tobacco. Camp buildings were rickety, meant to be temporary, built for utility, not comfort. The summers were sweltering, the winters were frigid, and each season's air crept in through the cracks to remind the lumbermen of their humanity. Felled trees were floated down the rivers (and later also transported with trains) to sawmills where they were cut for market. After clearing an area, the lumbermen picked up and moved on, leaving large, desolate spaces where forests had grown for ages.

During the 1920s, in the winding down of the lumber boom, when so many of the establishments that sprang up around the sawmills were becoming ghost towns, Raymond and Hortense Overholzer moved to northern Michigan. Mr. Overholzer was a hunter and taxidermist with a proclivity for woodworking, and he built a cabin from white pine on the Pere Marquette River in what would become the Manistee National Forest. The white pine in Michigan was harvested almost to extinction, and the Overholzers collected roots and stumps left over from the lumbermen. They spent the rest of their days (into the 1950s) dedicated to handcrafting their home with remnants of the pine forests that once stood in the area. Today, the cabin is a museum. There are more than 200 pieces - ottomans, dressers, chests, desks, chairs, candelabras, chandeliers, sconces, bed frames, a spinning gun rack, and a poker table with a hidden drawer above the lap of Mr. Overholzer's chair, where it is said he kept a secret ace. Every item of decorum or function was cut, carved, inlaid, nuanced, and fashioned by hand from pieces of white pine. For everything Mr. Overholzer made, Mrs. Overholzer wrote descriptions on scraps of paper.

The creation of the Forest Service (1905) and the establishment of the Manistee National Forest (1938) ushered our past of life in the woods into a new century while Michigan's southeast was creating work in factories that went on to supply cars to the country in the same dominant fashion as its forests supplied timber. Though timber is still a crucial industry, the way the forests are harvested today comes with a touch of maintenance and efforts of restoration, which were missing from the lumber heyday. The cabin was an expression of what much of Michigan's population was feeling in the early years of the 20th Century. The state was simultaneously holding onto its past in the forest and embracing its re-establishment as a giant of production in the quickly rising auto industry. As the Overholzers added to their collection, the National Forests in Michigan were rising up into the majestic spaces of tranquility and peace we enjoy today. In the Overholzers' own time, people heard stories about the cabin, and folks came to see if the rumor was true, if there really was a Shrine of the Pines.

This project began as an opportunity to create narrative poetry. At the start, I recalled famous Michigan stories I've heard all my life. Then, with a little research, I encountered a bunch of stories that were not so familiar to me. I had a mix of myths, legends, and folklore from all over the state. I began tackling my pile of stories in order of which were most fascinating to me, researching them further and rendering them into original poems. Despite the collection being made of myths, legends, and folklore, there is history in these poems, so they are best presented in a way that reveals a glimpse into the greater story of Michigan's past. As the process went on, it became increasingly clear that the table of contents should be ordered chronologically, as best as possible, using context clues when concrete dates were unavailable (which was most of the time), not randomly or in the order in which I wrote them. With so many poems contemporaneous to one another, the "chronological order" is more concerned with stacking poems in their historical periods than by exact years.

The first six poems predate the United States. Poems 1, 2, and 3 predate even recorded history, inspired by tales told in Michigan's oral tradition long before the Age of Exploration ushered in the colonial era. They are the most ancient stories in this collection, and they belong to the Native People of the Great Lakes Region. Poems 4, 5, and 6 move through the period of Michigan's history that records the days of trade between the Natives of the Great Lakes and the French. Trade led to settlement and colonization, which led to vast regions of what is now the United States and Canada being used as a theater of war for conflicts to play out between the French and English. The rest of the poems are the aftermath. They come from Michigan's first 100 years of statehood (from the middle of the 19th Century through the first few decades of the 20th) and depict the lore that came out of the occupational work during those early days of boom and bust. That is, the life of the lumberjack, the miner, the mariner, the railroader, the clerk, the farmer, the housewife, the lighthouse keeper, etc. The poems took on new meaning when I thought of them as belonging to distinct periods of Michigan's history. They remained a collection of stories from the state of Michigan, but, contextualized by the historical moments that produced them, also became a collection that tells the story of Michigan's inhabitants over a long period of time.

After viewing the poems ordered in this way, I had the scholarly urge to postpone publishing what I have here and keep adding. There are so many more stories in Michigan's history that are fit to be poems, that have a place scattered amongst the greater timeline. Seeing the poems ordered on the historical timeline illuminated how much is missing, and how much more these two peninsulas might rhyme. I subdued the urge to withhold what I have and move forward with the promise to myself that I will return to it and keep adding. I believe I have begun a project that I will come back to for a very long time.

Vincent Moyet
Alcona County, MI

Sources

Brunvand, Jan Harold. *The Study of American Folklore.* 4th ed.,
  W.W. Norton & Company Incorporated, 1998.

"Death of Con Culhane." *Genealogy Trails History Group: Chippewa
  County Michigan Genealogy & History* (contributed by Paul Petosky),
  genealogytrails.com/mich/chippewa/newsculhane.html.

Dorson, Richard Mercer. *Bloodstoppers & Bearwalkers.* Harvard
  University Press, 1978.

Dunbar, Willis Frederick, and George S. May. *Michigan: A History of
  the Wolverine State.* 3rd ed., Eerdmans, 1995.

Godfrey, Linda S. *Weird Michigan.* Sterling Publishing Company,
  Inc., 2006.

"Interview with Charles Sprague Taylor." *Northern Michigan University,*
  https://nmu.edu/upperpeninsulastudies/sites/upperpeninsulastudies/files/
  2021-11/Taylor_Charles_Sprague.pdf

James, Sheryl. *Michigan Legends.* University of Michigan Press,
  2013.

"Legends of Grosse Pointe." *Grosse Pointe Historical Society -
  Legends,* www.gphistorical.org/legends01.html.

"Railroad Logging." *Michigan State University,*
  https://project.geo.msu.edu/geogmich/RR-logging.html.

Schlosser, S.E. and Paul G. Hoffman. *Spooky Michigan: Tales of
  Hauntings, Strange Happenings, and Other Local Lore.* Globe Pequot, 2017.

Acknowledgements

My sister's illustrations make these poems tangible to the eye. This project is richer because of her participation.

My parents gave me the precious gifts of time and space to restructure my life as a writer. I am eternally grateful.

Vincent Moyet is a creative nonfiction and poetry writer. He earned a Master of Arts degree in English from DePaul University and a Bachelor of Arts degree in English and Religious Studies from Saint Xavier University. Vincent lives in the northeast of Michigan's Lower Peninsula.

Other Titles by Vincent Moyet

A Restaurant Story

Water

One Hundred Sober Thoughts

VM Publications

vincentmoyet.com